20TH CENTURY DESIGN

20s & 30s

BETWEEN THE WARS

For a free color catalog describing Gareth Stevens Publishing's list of high-quality books and multimedia programs, call 1-800-542-2595 (USA) or 1-800-461-9120 (Canada). Gareth Stevens Publishing's Fax: (414) 332-3567.

Library of Congress Cataloging-in-Publication Data available upon request from publisher. Fax: (414) 332-3567 for the attention of the Publishing Records Department.

ISBN 0-8368-2706-6

This North American edition first published in 2000 by
Gareth Stevens Publishing
A World Almanac Education Group Company
330 West Olive Street, Suite 100
Milwaukee, Wisconsin 53212 USA

Original edition © 1999 by David West Children's Books. First published in Great Britain in 1999 by Heinemann Library, Halley Court, Jordan Hill, Oxford OX2 8EJ, a division of Reed Educational and Professional Publishing Limited. This U.S. edition © 2000 by Gareth Stevens, Inc. Additional end matter © 2000 by Gareth Stevens, Inc.

Picture Research: Brooks Krikler Research

Gareth Stevens Senior Editor: Dorothy L. Gibbs
Gareth Stevens Series Editor: Christy Steele

Photo Credits:
Abbreviations: (t) top, (m) middle, (b) bottom, (l) left, (r) right

AKG London: pages 8(br), 14(t), 28(br).
Corbis: Cover (l, rm, mr), pages 3, 4-5, 5(tr, br), 10, 11(bl, br), 12(l), 13(both), 21(tl), 22(l), 22-23, 24(m), 25(b), 27(b) / Bettmann: pages 8(bl), 9(t), 23(bl), 24(t) / Edifice: page 8(t) / UPI: pages 12-13, 23(br).
Courtesy of the Kobal Collection / MGM: page 18(bl) / UFA: page 11(t) / Universal Pictures: Cover (tm), page 5(l).
Mary Evans Picture Library: pages 6(t, l), 7(l), 11(l), 12(r), 16(t), 16-17, 17(bl), 20(all), 26-27, 28(bl), 29(br).
Hulton Getty Collection: pages 4, 6(m), 9(b), 14(br), 15(t), 23(t), 28(tr).
Philip Jarrett: page 26(br).
Milepost 92 1/2: page 25(t).
Pictorial Press: page 22(b).
Science & Society Picture Library: pages 15(b), 18-19, 24(b), 26(bl) / National Railways Museum: Cover (br), page 29(bl).
Frank Spooner Pictures: page 21(br).
V&A Picture Library: Cover (tr), page 19.
Vitra Design Museum: Cover (bm), pages 14(bl), 16(b), 17(tr, br).
© Vogue/Condé Nast Publications Ltd. / Schiaparelli: page 7(r) / Steichen: page 6(br).
Reproduced by the kind permission of the London Transport Museum © London Regional Transport: page 28(tl).

Printed in Mexico

1 2 3 4 5 6 7 8 9 04 03 02 01 00

20TH CENTURY DESIGN

20s & 30s

BETWEEN THE WARS

Jackie Gaff

Gareth Stevens Publishing
A WORLD ALMANAC EDUCATION GROUP COMPANY

CONTENTS

Art deco was the reigning artistic style of the 1920s and 1930s. This sculpture from the Parisian music hall the Folies-Bergère is a striking example of art deco's stylized shapes and geometric patterns.

When unemployment skyrocketed in the 1930s, breadlines formed by people waiting for food handouts were a common sight in cities around the world.

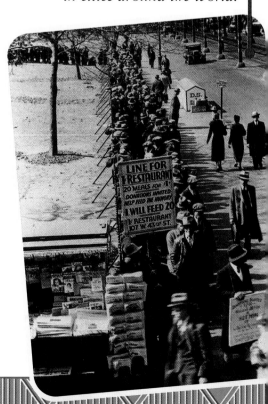

CHANGING TIMES

The 1920s and 1930s were decades of constant change and development. After the ravages of World War I (1914–1918), people struggled to forge a new era of peace and progress. The desire for a fresh start encouraged new ideas, and the challenge of using new materials to shape a modern way of life inspired architects and designers.

These two decades also saw changes in economics and politics, but the changes were not always for the better. In the early 1920s, many nations had to deal with large war debts and rising inflation. Then, in October 1929, Wall Street's New York Stock Exchange crashed, starting an economic depression that caused tremendous hardship — first in the United States, then throughout Europe.

As for politics, many countries were repressed under the authoritarian rule of powerful dictators. Fascism took hold under Benito Mussolini in Italy, Adolf Hitler in Germany, and Francisco Franco in Spain. The decades that began with so much optimism closed with the devastating turmoil of another world war.

During World War I, many women held jobs for the first time, prompting new financial and social independence for females. As women expressed their newfound freedom, hemlines rose, and clothing became simpler and more practical.

Designers gave a streamlined style to all forms of transportation, including steam trains like this 1938 Hudson J-3a.

The futuristic designs shown at the New York World's Fair in 1939 were the experimental climax of the postwar years.

FASHION

In the 1920s, women celebrated the financial and social freedoms they had earned during the war by inventing a totally new look. Now leading more active lives, women wanted clothing and hairstyles to match. As the fussiness of the prewar years dropped away, women cropped their hair into easy-to-manage, boyish bobs and began to wear shorter, loose-fitting garments that allowed far greater freedom of movement.

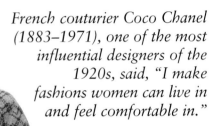

New athletic dance crazes, such as the Charleston, expressed the energy and freedom of the 1920s.

French couturier Coco Chanel (1883–1971), one of the most influential designers of the 1920s, said, "I make fashions women can live in and feel comfortable in."

Chanel's easy-to-wear look included dresses with dropped waists and cardigan jackets worn with pleated skirts.

Men also adopted more relaxed styles. Suits were cut looser and were made from softer fabrics.

FASHION FOR ALL

Wider availability accompanied the new look. A range of women's magazines and journals made discovering the latest fashion trends much easier, and sewing and knitting patterns, along with low-cost, department-store copies, made designer styles far more affordable.

MASS-PRODUCING RAYON

1 *Sheets of cellulose made from wood pulp are soaked in caustic soda.*

2 *The sheets are broken into fluffy flakes called cellulose crumbs.*

3 *The crumbs are aged for up to three days.*

4 *The crumbs are churned with the solvent carbon disulfide.*

5 *Caustic soda dissolves the crumb mixture to make viscose.*

6 *The viscose is aged and filtered.*

7 *The viscose is vacuum-treated to remove air bubbles.*

8 *The viscose is forced through spinnerets into a spin bath of sulfuric acid.*

9 *The finished rayon is wound onto spools.*

close-up of a spinneret

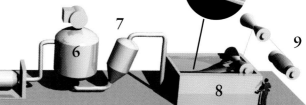

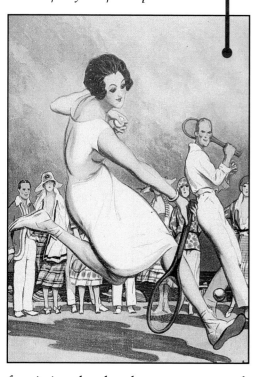

Tennis star Suzanne Lenglen exemplified the liberated look and lifestyle of the period.

MATERIAL GAINS

Fashion for all became even more possible with the mass production of rayon, the first artificial fabric. Rayon reproduced some of the luxury of silk at a fraction of the price. A variety of garments, from underwear to evening dresses, were made with rayon.

WOMANLY WAYS

By the late 1920s, styles that emphasized a sleek, feminine body shape were replacing the shapeless, boyish look. Hemlines dropped, and clothes were cut to cling to every curve. Streamlined fashions did not leave room for bulges, so many women "slimmed down" with lightweight girdles made of Lastex, a newly developed elastic fiber.

FANTASY FASHION

Italian-born Elsa Schiaparelli (1890–1973) was the most innovative fashion designer of the 1930s. Schiaparelli made some of her strangest creations with her friend, surrealist Salvador Dalí (1904–1989). These creations included a hat shaped like a shoe, a dress with a life-size red lobster design, and a jacket with lip-shaped pocket trim.

Schiaparelli's surreal hen hat (1938) had a bird's nest brim!

MODERNIST ARCHITECTURE

Simplicity was the key to architectural design in the 1920s. Radical architects of the postwar years reduced buildings to basic geometric shapes. Whenever possible, builders used prefabricated components to make construction work easier. These new buildings for the new age started a style that became known as modernism.

With its white concrete walls and metal-framed windows, this 1927 house is a classic modernist design.

SCHOOL OF THOUGHT

The Bauhaus design school in Germany was at the heart of modernism. German-born architect Walter Gropius (1883–1969) founded the school in 1919 to train artists how to design for industrial production. Bauhaus became as famous for its design theories as for its students. A primary Bauhaus theory was that form should follow function — the look of an object or building should be determined by its use or purpose.

LE CORBUSIER

Frenchman Le Corbusier (1887–1965), a radical architect fascinated by machines, declared that "the house is a machine for living in." He used reinforced concrete to construct the frameworks of his buildings, removing the need for weight-bearing walls and allowing for huge windows and open-plan interiors.

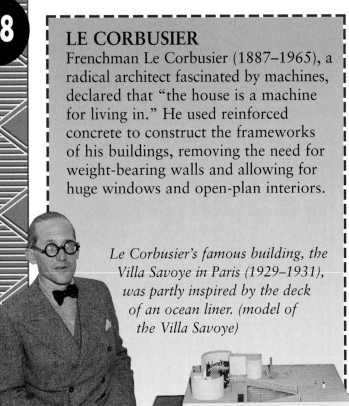

Le Corbusier's famous building, the Villa Savoye in Paris (1929–1931), was partly inspired by the deck of an ocean liner. (model of the Villa Savoye)

Walter Gropius, director of the Bauhaus school, designed the school's building in Dessau, Germany, in 1926.

8

SIMPLE TASTES

Keeping decoration to a minimum was one way to interpret the Bauhaus theory, and the work of leading modernist architects, such as Le Corbusier, Walter Gropius, and German-born Ludwig Mies van der Rohe (1886–1969), was certainly frill free. Their buildings generally had flat roofs, window frames prefabricated in metal (a lower-cost alternative to labor-intensive wood), and walls made of concrete. The form was plain and dominated by geometric shapes, such as cubes and rectangles.

MACHINES FOR LIVING

Buildings had become as streamlined and functional as a machine, the postwar symbol of speed and progress. The machine even stood for democracy; because mass production, usually by machine, made products more affordable, the products were available to more people.

Believing that everyone had the right to a well-designed house, leading modernist architects, including Walter Gropius and Le Corbusier, designed workers' homes at Weissenhofsiedlung in Stuttgart, Germany, in 1927.

BUCKMINSTER FULLER

Richard Buckminster Fuller (1895–1983), a trained engineer, was a wildly inventive American designer whose creative interests ranged from houses to cars. His architectural work bore no resemblance to the spare lines of modernist Le Corbusier's, yet Fuller was equally fascinated by machines and mass production. He applied the structural design of cars and aircraft to houses. His Dymaxion House (1927) was constructed of prefabricated units.

Buckminster Fuller and a model of his futuristic Dymaxion House

9

SKYSCRAPERS

Architects were inspired to do more than just design new houses. They wanted to reinvent entire cities, and the city of the future needed a special kind of building — the skyscraper.

PAVING THE WAY

Two 19th-century technological developments made skyscraper construction possible. First, a metal skeleton, designed to support walls as well as floors, was used in 1883 to build a Chicago skyscraper; then, in 1889, the electric elevator was invented.

10

New York City's Empire State Building was completed in 1931. At 1,250 feet (381 meters) high, it was the world's tallest building for forty years.

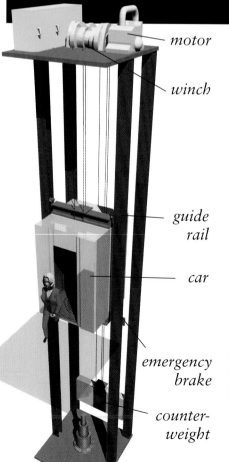

motor

winch

guide rail

car

emergency brake

counter-weight

GOING UP?

Modern elevators are either hydraulic (driven by the pressure of a liquid) or electric. Because hydraulic elevators are slower, they are not often used in skyscrapers. Today, the fastest electric elevators speed upward at about 2,000 feet (600 m) per minute. The car runs up and down on guide rails or in a guide tower. The electric motor does not pull the whole load; a counterweight rises as the car falls, then helps pull the car back up.

Without safety lines or helmets, construction workers risked their lives daily as they bolted and welded together steel sections of a skyscraper's framework — like pieces of a giant Erector set.

In Lang's futuristic Metropolis, *"sky bridges" connect a forest of gleaming skyscrapers.*

FUTURE WORLD

German director Fritz Lang's 1926 film *Metropolis* created a nightmarish future in which a large segment of the population lives as slaves. The film's message is that technology might pose a threat to humanity. Its amazing futuristic sets were inspired by a visit Lang made to New York City.

REACHING FOR THE SKIES

Although neither the skyscraper nor its technology was new, both truly came into their own in the 1920s. Architects designed more and more daring buildings that soared higher and higher into the skies — until the Wall Street Crash in 1929 interrupted the skyscraper boom.

JEWELS IN THE CROWN

Two of the most stunning skyscrapers were built in New York City. The 1,050-foot (320-m) Chrysler Building, designed by William Van Alen (1883–1954), was completed in 1930. Although commissioned by the Chrysler Corporation, the company never used the building, but its fabulous art deco crown was inspired by Chrysler car designs. It was the world's tallest building until the record was broken in 1931 by the 1,250-foot (381-m) Empire State Building, designed by Richmond H. Shreve (1877–1946), William Lamb (1883–1952), and Arthur Loomis Harmon (1878–1958).

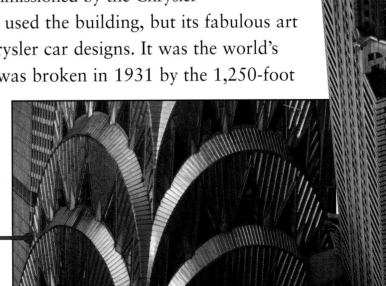

The top of New York City's Chrysler Building (1928–1930) was coated with steel, one of the most popular building materials of the time.

ART DECO STYLE

Art deco was the decorative style of the 1920s and 1930s. In contrast to the curling plant and animal motifs of art nouveau, art deco was sharp-edged and abstract. Colors were hot and vibrant, and geometric shapes dominated its patterns. Artists were inspired by civilizations considered exotic at the time — ancient Egyptians, Aztecs, Mayans, and tribal Africans.

The discovery of Tutankhamen's tomb in 1922 created a craze for all things Egyptian.

ART DECO DECOR

Favorite art deco motifs were pyramids, fans, sun rays, lightning flashes, and chevrons, as well as stylized waves, flowers, palm trees, cars, planes, and trains. Designers used these motifs to decorate public buildings, such as theaters and restaurants, but the designs also influenced the decors of suburban homes in the 1930s. The sun-ray motif was often used on gates, windows, and doors.

These elevator doors in the Chrysler Building are the epitome of art deco luxury. Costly wood veneer and metal inlays create an Egyptian lotus-flower motif. (William Van Alen, 1928–1930)

The French ocean liner Normandie (1932) glittered with art deco style. Its designer and craftsman Jean Dunand (1877–1942) created these lacquered panels.

Both the interior and exterior of the Chanin Building in New York (1929) were designed with art deco motifs. This executive-suite bathroom has geometric patterns with metal and glass detailing.

FOCUS POINT

Art deco got its name from *Exposition Internationale des Arts Décoratifs et Industriels Modernes*, an international exhibition of decorative arts held in Paris in 1925. With people from all over the world in attendance, the exhibition played a huge role in defining art deco and spreading its influence. The style did not begin immediately, but grew gradually.

The severe, modernist shape of the Hoover Factory in London was softened by Egyptian-style art deco, designed by Wallis, Gilbert & Partners in 1933.

LIGHT FANTASTIC

Modernist rooms were spacious, free of clutter, and filled with light that streamed in through huge windows, poured out from electrical fixtures, and bounced off white walls, mirrors, and chrome or stainless-steel furnishings.

TURNING ON THE POWER

Electric light was still an icon of modernness in the postwar years. Although the first power stations went into operation in London and New York City in 1882, it was some time before governments established national grid systems and before low-cost electricity became available to most people's homes.

14

Bauhaus director Walter Gropius designed his office as a showcase for the school. With its stark geometric shapes and patterns, the style is severely modernist.

PAINTING WITH LIGHT

Art deco designers used electric lighting, mirrors, and glass almost like paint or wallpaper. They made shimmering interiors for hotels, theaters, office buildings, and even the new luxury ocean liners that were being constructed in the post-war years. Usually lightbulbs were hidden inside uplighters or, sometimes, behind huge glass panels.

This table lamp greatly interested designers of the period. It was created in 1923–1924 by two Bauhaus students, Wilhelm Wagenfeld and K.J. Tucker. Copies are still being produced today.

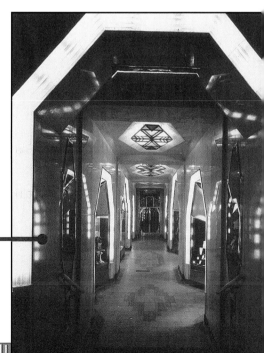

Hotel interiors were glittering display cases for the new look. (The Strand Palace Hotel in London, 1930)

LIGHT SCULPTURES

Not all designers, however, wanted to hide technology; some of the modernists deliberately incorporated it into their designs. They saw lightbulbs as more than simply objects for producing light; lightbulbs had their own artistic appeal. In the early 1920s, Dutch architect and furniture designer Gerrit Rietveld (1888–1964) pioneered the artistic use of lighting by creating sculptured fixtures using tube-shaped lightbulbs. The impressive lamp that hung in Walter Gropius's Bauhaus office was based on a Rietveld design.

Nations competed to create the world's fastest and most luxurious ocean liners, and ship interiors displayed the very latest in design.

LEADING LIGHT

The Anglepoise lamp, created in 1932, is still produced today. Its designer, George Carwardine (1887–1948), was an auto engineer. Carwardine based the movement of the lamp on that of the human arm, deliberately designing the original lacquered-steel and Bakelite lamp for mass production by Britain's Herbert Terry & Sons.

This poster promoted the Anglepoise lamp.

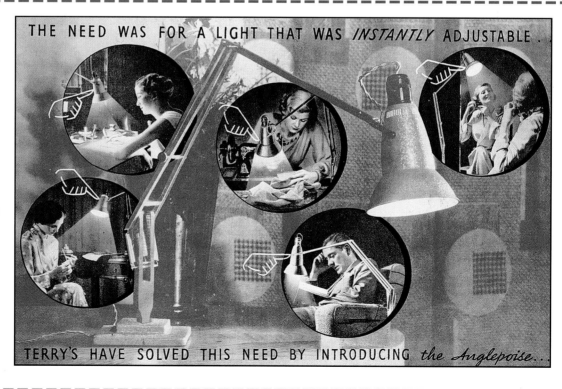

THE NEED WAS FOR A LIGHT THAT WAS *INSTANTLY* ADJUSTABLE .

TERRY'S HAVE SOLVED THIS NEED BY INTRODUCING *the Anglepoise*..

FURNITURE

An exciting development of the postwar years was the focus on designing objects deliberately for mass production. Until this time, most furniture was handcrafted. In the 1920s, however, designers started using materials, such as plywood, which could be turned into sleek, modernist furniture on factory production lines.

Not all new furniture was mass-produced. Modern designs, especially from wood, were also handcrafted.

16

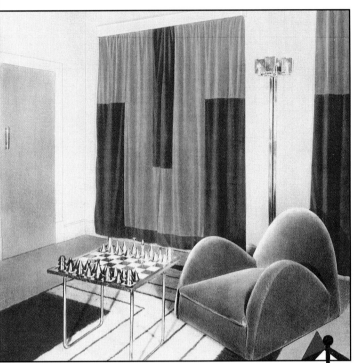

Fabrics with geometric shapes, a chess table made of metal and glass, and an abstract armchair create a stylish art deco room.

WOODWORKING SKILLS

The technology for bending wood was developed in the 18th century, but it was not until the 1920s that Alvar Aalto (1898–1976) of Finland first saw its potential for modernist design. Aalto and his wife, Aino Marsio, experimented with both bent wood and plywood. Aalto's first piece, the Paimio chair, was perfected by the early 1930s.

A BONDING RELATIONSHIP

In 1841, German furniture-maker Michael Thonet (1796–1871) patented the technology for bending wood. Thin sheets of wood, called veneers, are glued together and compressed to laminate, or bond, them. Then steam is used to bend them. Plywood, developed later, is stronger. To make plywood, the grain of each new sheet of veneer runs in the opposite direction of the sheet underneath.

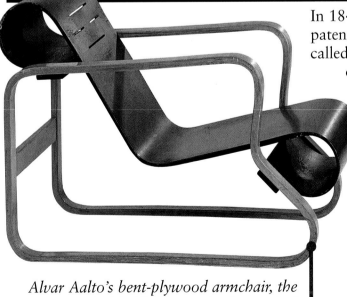

Alvar Aalto's bent-plywood armchair, the Paimio (1931–1932), was both practical to produce and fairly comfortable.

The veneers are glued and compressed.

The plywood is bent by steam.

Sheets of plywood veneer are laid crosswise.

The simple design and construction of Marcel Breuer's tubular-steel Model B3 chair (1925) made it ideal for airy, open-plan, modernist rooms.

MACHINE-AGE MATERIALS

Some modernist designers were inspired by metals, such as steel and aluminum, which were used mainly in the construction industry. Hungarian-born Marcel Breuer (1902–1981) was a pioneer in designing with metals. Breuer trained at the Bauhaus School, where, at first, he spent most of his time working with wood. In 1925, however, Breuer was so impressed by the strength and lightness of his new Adler bicycle's tubular-steel frame that he made up his mind to apply the same techniques in making furniture. Breuer's Model B3 revolutionized the design of the armchair. The Model B3 was made of tubular steel and leather, and, unlike the heavy, bulky, upholstered armchairs of the past, it was simple, lightweight, and strong.

Many modernist designs are still in production today, including this outdoor chair called the Landi. It was created in 1938 by Swiss designer Hans Coray (b. 1906) and is made from an aluminum alloy.

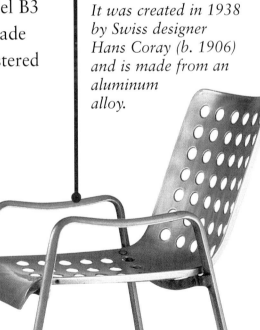

Cube-shaped, leather armchairs; a metal-and-leather footstool; and the strong, vertical and horizontal lines of the designs in this 1930s sitting room are typically modernist.

DECO HOMES

In its early years, art deco stood for quality and luxury. Artists used expensive materials to make handcrafted goods. Art deco furniture, for example, was usually made of lacquered wood with bronze or chrome frames, snakeskin or sharkskin coverings, and inlays of exotic ebony, rosewood, or mother-of-pearl. As art deco designs grew more popular, lower-priced versions became available.

18

The brightly colored ceramics of British designer Clarice Cliff (1899–1972) were pure art deco — at affordable prices.

AT HOME WITH ART DECO

In the 1930s, art deco designs trickled into every corner of the home, affecting items from curtains to radios. The trickle became a torrent when mass production flooded the market with inexpensive objects made from the new plastics, Bakelite and Perspex.

THE MAGIC OF THE MOVIES

The 1920s and 1930s were growth years for the film industry. When the first successful talkie, *The Jazz Singer*, was released in 1927, more than fifty million people were already going to films regularly each year. Costumes and set designs helped introduce art deco styles to most of the population.

Aztec and Mayan designs inspired the art deco sets for the 1929 film The Kiss.

This art deco coffee table is laden with art deco glass ornaments.

PLASTIC FANTASTIC

Invented in 1907 by Belgian-born chemist Leo Baekeland, Bakelite was the first industrially important plastic. It was initially used as an alternative to rubber for insulating electrical plugs and switches. By the 1920s, however, designers recognized its greater potential. Bakelite had the shiny look modern designers loved, and it came in a range of opaque or see-through colors — butterscotch yellow, scarlet red, violet blue, lime green, and orange, as well as brown and black. Before long, everything from clocks, radios, and jukeboxes to buttons, hairbrushes, and jewelry were made from Bakelite.

FAKE GLASS

Perspex, developed in 1928, was first sold in the 1930s. This new plastic looked just like glass but was lighter in weight and much harder to break. In later years, Perspex was used to make windshields for cars and airplanes.

From candlesticks to salt-and-pepper shakers, 1930s table ornaments were made from Perspex, a plastic that could be either opaque or transparent.

THE PRODUCTION OF PLASTIC

Because Bakelite could be cast and molded by machine, it was easily mass-produced. It is made from two chemicals, phenol and formaldehyde, which solidify into a hard resin when heated. Any color can be added to the mixture before molding, and mixing two colors creates a marbled effect.

Liquid phenol and formaldehyde are poured into a steel mold.

The mold is baked in an oven.

The solid Bakelite form is removed from the mold.

Before the Bakelite Ekco AD65 hit the market in 1934, radios came in square, wooden boxes. British architect Wells Coates (1895–1958) created this revolutionary design.

KITCHENWARE

In spite of massive unemployment during the 1920s and 1930s, the standard of living for people who did have jobs had rarely been so good. Rising living standards led to increasing demands for consumer goods.

Although women earned new freedoms during World War I, the majority remained full-time homemakers and mothers.

FEEDING THE DEMAND

As more and more homes were connected to electricity, inventors created all sorts of appliances — from electric kettles and irons to vacuum cleaners, hair dryers, and electric razors — that used this new power source. Manufacturers knew that the excitement over products just because they were electric would quickly wear off, so they modified and updated designs regularly to expand the market for these products. Even when the gadgets were not new, they looked new — and consumers wanted the new look.

This page from a 1939 department store catalog shows the wide range of electrical products for sale.

DESIGNING FOR INDUSTRY

German architect and designer Peter Behrens (1868–1940) was probably the first artist to apply his skills to industrial design. In 1907, Behrens began advising AEG, a German electrical company. By the early 1930s, however, with the American economy recovering from the Wall Street Crash of 1929, the United States was leading the world in the design and production of industrial goods.

British pottery manufacturer T.G. Green introduced cheap but functional Cornish Kitchenware in 1927, when the jobs of its factory workers were threatened by a declining economy.

Made of shiny Bakelite and metal, the Moka Express is an art deco classic. It was designed in 1930 but was not mass-produced until after World War II (1939–1945).

MODERN KITCHENS

If the modern home was a machine for living, then its kitchen was a laboratory for the scientific preparation and storage of food. Above all else, kitchens had to be streamlined and hygienic. By the 1930s, sleek, new built-ins were replacing old free-standing cupboards, and metal stoves and refrigerators were coated with enamel for easy cleaning. Industrial designers left no piece of kitchenware untouched. They restyled everything — toasters, food mixers, crockery, cutlery, saucepans, even kitchen trays, clocks, and radios — to give the entire kitchen the new look.

Postwar designers created the shiny surfaces they loved by coating metals either with enamel or with another metal, such as chrome. Enamel is powdered glass that is heated until it melts onto the metal. A metal is coated with chrome using a process called electroplating. When an electric current is passed through a solution containing chrome, positive chrome ions are attracted to a negative cathode, and a thin layer is deposited on the object being plated.

An electric current travels from cathode to anode.

anode (+)

cathode (-) attached to the object to be plated

Positive chrome ions are attracted to the cathode.

solution containing chrome ions

21

Swedish engineer Gustaf Dalén (1869–1937) designed the Aga oven in 1922. At the time, the oven's clean lines were on the cutting edge of modernism.

Raymond Loewy (1893–1986) was one of the United States' leading industrial designers. He restyled everything from cars to Coca-Cola bottles. His Coldspot Super Six refrigerator (1935) was one of the first consumer products with a sleek, streamlined shape.

ROAD MACHINES

Mass-production techniques were developed during the 19th century, but not until 1913, when American Henry Ford put an assembly line in his automobile factory, did manufacturing become truly efficient. Ford's assembly line enabled him to drop the price of a Model T from $950 in 1908 to less than $300 by the mid 1920s.

Raymond Loewy restyled Greyhound buses in 1940. The banded bodywork created a stream-lined look and added to the illusion of speed.

RIDING IN STYLE

With about fifteen million Model Ts sold by the mid 1920s, the Ford Motor Company had completely cornered the market for family cars. Later that decade, however, Ford's stranglehold would be broken by a new technique known as "styling." In 1927, General Motors made engineer Harley Earl (1893–1969) head of its new Art and Color Section. For the next thirty-two years, Earl was responsible for the design of all General Motors cars. While Model Ts were always black and still looked exactly the same as they had in 1908, Earl believed a car should be visually appealing, or stylish. He also began the practice of introducing a new design as soon as an old model's appeal wore off.

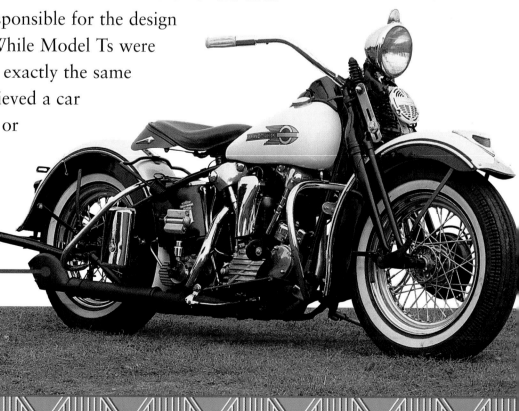

The stretched body and sleek chromework of this 1939 Harley-Davidson motorcycle screams speed. (first model built in 1903)

22

Designed by Carl Breer, the Chrysler Airflow (1934) was one of the first streamlined cars.

THE SHAPE OF SPEED

A stylish car had to look modern, and speed was one of the key symbols of postwar modernness. Engineers had learned that machines move faster if they have a smooth, streamlined shape, so industrial designers streamlined everything in sight — even objects like pencil sharpeners. When it came to road machines, streamlining meant curved bodies, bumpers, and radiators along with slanted windshields and sleek, shiny chromework.

THE PEOPLE'S CARS

Many countries adopted Henry Ford's idea of creating affordable family cars. In 1934, German dictator Adolf Hitler (1889–1945) asked Ferdinand Porsche (1875–1951) to design a *volkswagen*, or "people's car," which was later called the Beetle. Pierre Boulanger (1886–1950) designed the French Citroën 2CV in 1939, and Alec Issigonis (1906–1988) created the British Mini in 1959.

Adolf Hitler attended the opening of the first Volkswagen plant in 1938.

GOING WITH THE FLOW

When a machine moves, the resistance of the air or water it travels through slows it down. This resistance is called drag. Reducing drag makes machines move faster and use less fuel. Streamlining is shaping an object to reduce drag. Smooth curves help, but the ideal streamlined shape is a teardrop. A few industrial designers, including Americans Buckminster Fuller and Norman Bel Geddes (1893–1958), designed teardrop-shaped vehicles, but most of their designs were considered too futuristic to put into mass production.

Buckminster Fuller's three-wheeled Dymaxion car (1933–1934) is a fine example of the streamlined, teardrop shape.

Norman Bel Geddes, in 1939, with a model of one of his futuristic designs, a teardrop-shaped bus

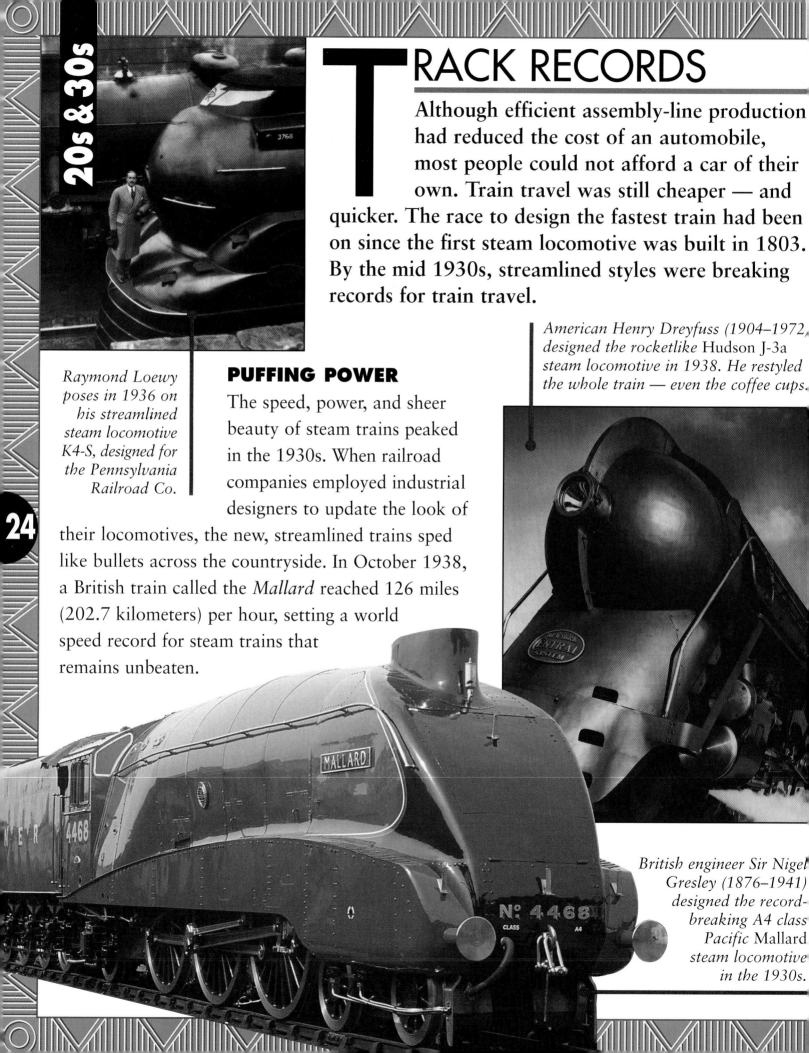

TRACK RECORDS

Although efficient assembly-line production had reduced the cost of an automobile, most people could not afford a car of their own. Train travel was still cheaper — and quicker. The race to design the fastest train had been on since the first steam locomotive was built in 1803. By the mid 1930s, streamlined styles were breaking records for train travel.

Raymond Loewy poses in 1936 on his streamlined steam locomotive K4-S, designed for the Pennsylvania Railroad Co.

24

PUFFING POWER

The speed, power, and sheer beauty of steam trains peaked in the 1930s. When railroad companies employed industrial designers to update the look of their locomotives, the new, streamlined trains sped like bullets across the countryside. In October 1938, a British train called the *Mallard* reached 126 miles (202.7 kilometers) per hour, setting a world speed record for steam trains that remains unbeaten.

American Henry Dreyfuss (1904–1972) designed the rocketlike Hudson J-3a steam locomotive in 1938. He restyled the whole train — even the coffee cups.

British engineer Sir Nigel Gresley (1876–1941) designed the record-breaking A4 class Pacific Mallard steam locomotive in the 1930s.

HIGH-STYLE RESTYLING

Designers, particularly in the United States, also restyled train interiors. American train travelers found themselves relaxing in plush armchairs in air-conditioned compartments, or they could visit an open-view observation car or have a drink in a chrome-plated cocktail lounge.

THE END OF AN ERA

The days of coal-fueled steam trains were numbered, however, when nations switched to cleaner, electric-powered rail systems. An electric train was first demonstrated in 1879. By the 1930s, electric trains were widespread in Europe, particularly in countries such as Switzerland and Norway, where hydroelectric power stations pumped out low-cost, renewable, pollution-free energy.

THE RISE OF DIESEL-ELECTRIC TRAINS

Cleaner, more fuel-efficient, diesel-electric trains first ran in the 1930s. Whereas steam engines converted less than ten percent of their messy coal fuel into hauling power, diesel-electric engines converted more than twenty-five percent of their non-polluting fuel into power. The diesel engine drives an electric generator, which powers traction motors, spaced along the entire length of the train, that turn the wheels.

Germany's two-car Flying Hamburger was one of the first diesel-electric trains. Its speed on its first run in Köln in 1932 averaged 78 miles (126 km) per hour.

Pioneer Zephyr *(1934) was the first American diesel-electric train. It was also the first to have a shiny, stainless-steel body. Its top speed was 110 miles (177 km) per hour.*

HIGH FLYERS

The 1920s and 1930s were decades of "firsts" for aviators. Charles Lindbergh made history in 1927 when he completed the first solo flight across the Atlantic Ocean. Just one year later, Charles Smith and C.T. Ulm made the first transpacific flight. In 1932, Amelia Earhart became the first woman to complete a solo Atlantic crossing.

ONWARD AND UPWARD

Sports flying became popular, too. Aviators competed to win cash prizes and trophies for flying higher and faster than ever before. Competitors in the international Schneider Trophy races for seaplanes set many important speed records. The world airspeed record went from 281 miles (452 km) per hour in 1923 to 428 miles (689 km) per hour in 1931. The race to be the fastest in the air brought new technological breakthroughs as engineers worked to create lighter, streamlined planes.

In the mid-1930s, customers of Imperial Airways, the British national airline, were still flying in slow, bulky biplanes.

The British team flying this Supermarine S-6B seaplane won the 1931 Schneider Trophy. The streamlined design of the S-6B influenced the design of the World War II Spitfire.

PIGGYBACK LIFTOFF

The greatest obstacle to transatlantic passenger flights was designing an airliner that could carry enough fuel. British engineer Major Robert Mayo came up with one solution — reducing the amount of fuel needed for takeoff. He used a large, powerful flying boat to help launch a smaller plane into the air. Once airborne, the smaller plane could make a long journey with little fuel.

Mayo's plane made its only Atlantic crossing in 1939.

With its upholstered seats, luggage racks, and curtains, the cabin of a 1934 airliner offered passengers comfort and luxury. Passengers on the first airliners sat on wicker chairs and fought off the cold with overcoats and hot-water bottles.

SPREADING THE LOAD

Early planes were made mainly of wood and canvas. Although they were light, they were neither streamlined nor strong. Experiments with streamlined metal designs began during World War I, and the early 1920s saw a revolutionary new way of making "stressed-skin" aircraft with duralumin, a lightweight aluminum alloy developed in 1908–1912.

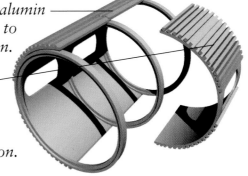

A skin of thin duralumin sheets was riveted to the plane's skeleton.

The stressed-skin handled much of the load previously carried only by the skeleton.

GAINING THE FREEDOM OF THE SKIES

Until 1919, the skies belonged mainly to pilots. Only a few lucky passengers had ever traveled by plane. When regular passenger flights began after World War I, planes were noisy, converted bombers. Not until the mid 1920s, when the first large, national airline companies were founded, was enough money available to invest in new passenger airliners. Many of the early airliners were flying boats because few landing strips existed outside Europe and the United States. As technological breakthroughs, such as stressed-skin structure, were adopted, the shape of airliners evolved from boxy, biwinged planes into streamlined monoplanes.

Designed in 1935 by engineer Arthur E. Raymond for the American Douglas Company, the Douglas DC-3 had the most modern, streamlined, stressed-skin structure. The DC-3 became the world's most successful airliner.

POSTERS & PACKAGING

PEfficient mass production created the need for mass marketing, and an awareness of the importance of advertising grew in post-war years. In the United States, a number of professional advertising agencies were started on New York City's Madison Avenue in the 1920s.

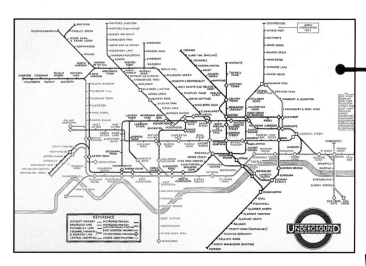

British engineering draftsman Henry C. Beck (1901–1974) based the abstract, geometric design of his map of the 1933 London Underground on electrical-circuit diagrams.

Frenchman Paul Colin (1892–1985) designed this poster for a 1925 show that introduced Europe to the music of black Americans.

28

AT THE STROKE OF A PEN

The design of posters and packaging had to be as current as the goods and services they advertised. The 1920s saw a creative explosion of sans-serif typefaces, particularly from Bauhaus designers, such as Herbert Bayer (1900–1985). These typefaces looked clean, modern, and streamlined.

British railroad companies commissioned contemporary artists to create a series of striking advertisements.

Illustrated Booklet free from Passenger Managers, Liverpool Street Station, London, E.C.2, LNER York Waverley Station, Edinburgh; Traffic Superintendent, LNER, Aberdeen, or any LNER Enquiry Office.

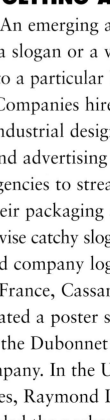

The message of this 1931 poster for a German shipping line is that taking an ocean voyage is as fashionable as cropped hair and a cloche!

BUT IS IT ART?

In the 1920s, most magazines were illustrated. People debated as to whether photographs were art. Photographs grew in popularity, however, when magazines began to tell stories through photo-essays.

The British photo-essay magazine Picture Post *debuted in 1938.*

THE PLEASURES OF TRAVEL

In the 1920s, very few people thought of traveling any great distance for a pleasure trip until transportation companies began to advertise their services. French graphic artist A.M. Cassandre (1901–1968) created some of the most striking posters of this period. Cassandre's clean, sans-serif typography; strong colors; and stylized artwork greatly influenced graphic designers throughout the world.

GETTING A MESSAGE ACROSS

An emerging advertising trend was using a slogan or a visual logo to build loyalty to a particular brand. Companies hired industrial designers and advertising agencies to streamline their packaging and devise catchy slogans and company logos. In France, Cassandre created a poster series for the Dubonnet company. In the United States, Raymond Loewy restyled the packaging for the Lucky Strike company.

29

Cassandre's 1927 poster promoting the streamlined Etoile du Nord *train is one of the world's best-known advertisements.*

In Britain, posters tried to sell the idea that Guinness ale was good for you.

· T I M E   L I N E ·

	DESIGN	WORLD EVENTS	TECHNOLOGY	FAMOUS PEOPLE	ART & MEDIA
1920	•Chanel: "yachting pants" for women	•U.S.: women get vote	•First electric hair dryer	•Joan of Arc canonized	•D.H. Lawrence: Women in Love
1921	•Chanel No. 5 perfume launched	•Chinese communist party founded	•Insulin discovered	•Marie Stopes opens Britain's first birth control clinic	•Rudolph Valentino stars in The Sheik
1922	•Dalén: Aga oven	•Russia becomes USSR	•Choc-ice (Eskimo pies)	•Tutankhamen's tomb opened	•James Joyce: Ulysses •T.S. Eliot: The Wasteland
1923		•Italy: Mussolini seizes power	•Autogiro (early helicopter) flown in Spain		•Cecil B. de Mille: The Ten Commandments
1924	•Rietveld: exposed-lightbulb sculptured lamp	•Britain: first Labour government elected	•Rayon named •Italy: first superhighway opens	•Lenin dies	•Gershwin: Rhapsody in Blue
1925	•Paris exhibition of decorative arts		•Scotch tape	•George Bernard Shaw wins Nobel Prize for Literature	•F. Scott Fitzgerald: The Great Gatsby
1926	•Breuer: B32 (Cesca) tubular-steel chair	•Britain: General Strike	•J.L. Baird: first television •Goddard: first rocket	•Ederle swims the English Channel •Valentino dies	•Fritz Lang: Metropolis
1927	•Buckminster Fuller: Dymaxion House	•German stock market collapses	•First Volvo car •Polyesters first used	•Charles Lindbergh: first solo flight across Atlantic	•First successful "talkie": The Jazz Singer
1928		•USSR: Stalin's first five-year plan	•Penicillin discovered •Perspex developed	•Emeline Pankhurst dies	•Walt Disney: first Mickey Mouse cartoon
1929	•Schiaparelli's first full collection	•U.S.: Wall Street Crash		•U.S.: Hoover elected president	•Mondrian: Composition in a Square
1930	•Van Alen's Chrysler Building completed	•India: Gandhi leads Salt March protest	•Planet Pluto identified •Turbojet engine patented	•Amy Johnson: first woman to fly to Australia	•Marlene Dietrich stars in The Blue Angel
1931	•Le Corbusier: Villa Savoye	•Japanese army occupies Chinese Manchuria	•Lastex yarn introduced		•Dalí: Limp Watches •Cagney in The Public Enemy
1932	•Carwardine: Anglepoise lamp	•Nazis take control of Reichstag (parliament)	•Polyethylene created •First radio telescope	•Amelia Earhart flies solo across Atlantic	•Huxley: Brave New World
1933	•Bauhaus design school closed by Nazis	•Hitler in power as Chancellor of Germany	•Lemaître proposes Big Bang theory		•Fay Wray in King Kong •Garbo in Queen Christina
1934	•Wells Coates: Ekco AD65 radio	•China: Mao leads communists on Long March	•Nylon •Cat's-eye road studs first used	•Shirley Temple wins an Oscar at age six	•Henry Miller: Tropic of Cancer
1935	•Douglas DC3 •Loewy: Coldspot refrigerator	•Italy invades Abyssinia (Ethiopia)	•Germany: first TV broadcasting station built	•Malcolm Campbell sets 300 mph land speed record	•Astaire and Rogers star in Top Hat
1936	•Volkswagen Beetle designed by Porsche	•Spanish Civil War begins •Edward VIII abdicates		•Jessie Owens stars at Berlin Olympics	•Ben Nicholson: White Relief
1937		•India: Congress Party wins elections	•Ballpoint pen •Polyurethanes discovered		•Picasso: Guernica •Walt Disney: Snow White
1938	•Dreyfuss: streamlined Hudson J-3a train	•Germany and Austria unite (Anschluss)	•Teflon discovered		•Moore: Recumbent Figure •First Superman comic strip
1939	•New York World's Fair	•Spanish Civil War ends •World War II begins	•Heinkel built first jet aircraft	•Sigmund Freud dies	•John Steinbeck: The Grapes of Wrath

GLOSSARY

art deco: a design style that features angular, geometric shapes and brilliant colors.

art nouveau: a design style that features plant and flower forms with graceful, curving lines.

Bakelite: the trade name for the first, widely used synthetic plastic.

chevrons: figures or patterns that have the shape of a *V* or an inverted *V*.

chrome: an alloy of the chemical element chromium, a strong, hard, steel-gray metal, which is used as a rust-resistant coating over steel or another metal.

cloche: a close-fitting ladies hat with a rounded crown, which was particularly fashionable in the 1920s worn over the popular cropped hairstyles.

industrial designer: a person who designs products that usually will be made by machines.

Lastex: the trade name for an elastic yarn consisting of a rubber core coated with silk, cotton, wool, or rayon.

Perspex: the trade name for a durable, lightweight, see-through plastic that looks like glass.

prefabricated: premade or manufactured as a unit of a larger construction, such as a wall, a window, a stairway, or a section of reinforced concrete for a building, for quick assembly at a construction site.

reinforced concrete: concrete strengthened by having steel bars or wires embedded in it.

surrealist: a person who produces fantastic, non-conforming, often bizarre, images or effects in works of art or literature.

uplighters: electrical lighting fixtures, often positioned at ground level, that focus light upward from a lightbulb inside the fixture.

MORE BOOKS TO READ

The 20s & 30s: Flappers & Vamps. 20th Century Fashion (series). Cally Blackman (Gareth Stevens)

Accept No Substitutes: The History of American Advertising. People's History (series). Christina B. Mierau (Lerner Publications)

America's Top 10 Skyscrapers. America's Top 10 (series). Edward Ricciuti (Blackbirch Marketing)

Art Deco Interiors: Decoration and Design Classics of the 1920s and 1930s. Patricia Bayer (Thames and Hudson)

Eyewitness: Trains. John Coiley (Dorling Kindersley)

Fashions of a Decade: The 1930s. Fashions of a Decade (series). Maria Constantino (Facts on File)

Great Discoveries & Inventions That Improved Transportation. Antonio Casanellas (Gareth Stevens)

Machines: Engines, Elevators, and X-Rays. Science @ Work (series). Janice Parker (Raintree/Steck-Vaughn)

Pioneers of the Air. Great Explorers (series). Molly Burkett (Barrons Juveniles)

The Roaring Twenties. Cornerstones of Freedom (series). R. Conrad Stein (Children's Press)

WEB SITES

Art Deco Architecture. *www.geocities.com/SoHo/Studios/1925/*

Bauhaus Weimar (1919–25) and Dessau (1925–33). *craton.geol.brocku.ca/guest/jurgen/bau1.htm*

Thonet Museum. *www.thonet.at/english/museum01.htm*

Time 100 Scientists & Thinkers: Chemist Leo Baekeland. *www.time.com/time/time100/scientist/ profile/baekeland.html*

Due to the dynamic nature of the Internet, some web sites stay current longer than others. To find additional web sites, use a reliable search engine with one or more of the following keywords: *Alvar Aalto, Anglepoise lamp, art deco, aviation, Bakelite, Bauhaus, Chanel, elevator, Buckminster Fuller, Raymond Loewy, Perspex, skyscrapers,* and *trains.*

INDEX

32